Rewards for Memorizing the Qur'aan

Compiled by Umm 'AbdirRahmaan Tara Hashim

بسم الله الرحمن الرحيم

Rewards for Memorizing the Qur'aan

First Edition: Jumaadah al Aakhir 1443AH – January 2022CE

Utrujjah Press

utrujjahpress@gmail.com

www.quraanteacherresources.blogspot.com
Instagram: @utrujjah_press

ISBN: 978-1-8380525-7-7

Contents

Introduction

This booklet was put together to remind students and their parents of the amazing rewards and status of those who memorize the Noble Book of Allaah, His uncreated Speech, the Qur'aan. It should be an incentive for those who haven't started the journey of memorization yet and also for those who are mid-way.

There is a mention of how to congratulate the memorizers at the end of the booklet.

Allaah grant us sincerity in everything that we do.

Allaah guide us to worship Him alone according to the pure sunnah.

Allaah grant us success to memorize the Noble Qur'aan, understand it how the Pious Predecessors understood it from the Prophet ﷺ, practice it and teach it to others aameen!

بسم الله الرحمن الرحيم

Rewards for Memorizing the Qur'aan and the Status of the one who Memorizes

Shaykhul Islaam Ibn Taymiyyah رحمه الله said,

"What is required from the Qur'aan is to understand its meanings and act upon it. If this is not the goal of the one memorizing it then he will not be from the People of Knowledge or Religion." (Majmoo' Fawtaawaa vol. 23 p55).

Rewards for the one who has Memorized the Qur'aan

1. A Person who recites the Qur'aan and learns it by heart will be with the Angels

Aa'ishah رضي الله عنها narrated that the Prophet صلى الله عليه وسلم said,

"Such a person as recites the Quran and masters it by heart, will be with the noble righteous scribes (in Heaven). And such a person exerts himself to learn the Quran by heart, and recites it with great difficulty, will have a double reward."

عَنْ عَائِشَةَ، عَنِ النَّبِيِّ صلى الله عليه وسلم قَالَ " مَثَلُ الَّذِي يَقْرَأُ الْقُرْآنَ وَهْوَ حَافِظٌ لَهُ مَعَ السَّفَرَةِ الْكِرَامِ الْبَرَرَةِ، وَمَثَلُ الَّذِي يَقْرَأُ الْقُرْآنَ وَهْوَ يَتَعَاهَدُهُ وَهْوَ عَلَيْهِ شَدِيدٌ، فَلَهُ أَجْرَانِ ".

(Saheeh al Bukhaaree no. 4937)

2. The Memorizer of the Qur'aan will be saved from the Fire

'Uqbah bin 'Aamir رضي الله عنه said I heard the Messenger of Allaah صلى الله عليه وسلم say, "If the Qur'aan was put in a skin (the memorizer of Qur'aan) then it was thrown into the Fire, it would not burn."

لَوْ جُعِلَ الْقُرْآنُ فِي إِهَابٍ، ثُمَّ أُلْقِيَ فِي النَّارِ، مَا احْتَرَقَ
(Daarimee; Silsilah Saheehah no. 3562).

3. **The Qur'aan will intercede on the Day of Resurrection and**
4. **Sooratul Baqarah and Aali 'Imraan will come as two clouds, flocks of birds or two shades**

Abu Umama رضي الله عنه said he heard Allah's Messenger (ﷺ) say:
"Recite the Qur'an, for on the Day of Resurrection it will come as an intercessor for those who recite It. Recite the two bright ones, al-Baqara and Surah Al 'Imran, for on the Day of Resurrection they will come as two clouds or two shades, or two flocks of birds in ranks, pleading for those who recite them. Recite Surah al-Baqara, for to take recourse to it is a blessing and to give it up is a cause of grief, and the magicians cannot confront it."

حَدَّثَنِي أَبُو أُمَامَةَ، الْبَاهِلِيُّ قَالَ سَمِعْتُ رَسُولَ اللَّهِ صلى الله عليه وسلم يَقُولُ " اقْرَءُوا الْقُرْآنَ فَإِنَّهُ يَأْتِي يَوْمَ الْقِيَامَةِ شَفِيعًا لأَصْحَابِهِ اقْرَءُوا الزَّهْرَاوَيْنِ الْبَقَرَةَ وَسُورَةَ آلِ عِمْرَانَ فَإِنَّهُمَا تَأْتِيَانِ يَوْمَ الْقِيَامَةِ كَأَنَّهُمَا غَمَامَتَانِ أَوْ كَأَنَّهُمَا غَيَايَتَانِ أَوْ كَأَنَّهُمَا فِرْقَانِ مِنْ طَيْرٍ صَوَافَّ تُحَاجَّانِ عَنْ أَصْحَابِهِمَا اقْرَءُوا سُورَةَ الْبَقَرَةِ فَإِنَّ أَخْذَهَا بَرَكَةٌ وَتَرْكَهَا حَسْرَةٌ وَلاَ تَسْتَطِيعُهَا الْبَطَلَةُ " .

(Saheeh Muslim 804a)

5. **He will receive good deeds for each letter he reads of the Qur'aan**

Narrated 'Abdullah bin Mas'ud رضي الله عنه 'The Messenger of Allah (ﷺ) said:
"Whoever recites a letter from Allah's Book, then he receives the reward from it, and the reward of ten the like of it. I do not say that Alif Lam Mim is a letter, but Alif is a letter, Lam is a letter and Mim is a letter."

قَالَ سَمِعْتُ عَبْدَ اللَّهِ بْنَ مَسْعُودٍ، يَقُولُ قَالَ رَسُولُ اللَّهِ صلى الله عليه وسلم " مَنْ قَرَأَ حَرْفًا مِنْ كِتَابِ اللَّهِ فَلَهُ بِهِ حَسَنَةٌ وَالْحَسَنَةُ بِعَشْرِ أَمْثَالِهَا لاَ أَقُولُ الم حَرْفٌ وَلَكِنْ أَلِفٌ حَرْفٌ وَلاَمٌ حَرْفٌ وَمِيمٌ حَرْفٌ "

(Tirmidhee 3158)

6. He will receive the same reward as those he has taught Qur'aan

Aboo Sahl al Qattaan رضي الله عنه said that the Prophet صلى الله عليه وسلم said,
"Whoever teaches an aayah from the Book of Allaah, the Mighty and Exalted, will get the same reward as the one who recites it."

عَنْ أَنَسٍ، قَالَ: قَالَ رَسُولُ اللَّهِ صَلَّى اللهُ عَلَيْهِ وَسَلَّمَ: «مَنْ عَلَّمَ آيَةً مِنْ كِتَابِ اللَّهِ كَانَ لَهُ ثَوَابُهَا مَا تُلِيَتْ»

(Silsilah Saheehah no. 1335).

7. Each Aayaah learned is better than getting a big humped she-camel

'Uqba bin 'Amir رضي الله عنه reported:
When we were in Suffa, the Messenger of Allah (ﷺ) came out and said: Which of you would like to go out every morning to Buthaan or al-'Aqiq and bring two large she-camels without being guilty of sin or without severing the ties of kinship? We said: Messenger of Allah, we would like to do it. Upon this he said: Does not one of you go out in the morning to the mosque and teach or recite two verses from the Book of Allah. the Majestic and Glorious? That is better for him than two she-camels, and three verses are better (than three she-camels) and four verses are better for him than four (she-camels), and so on with the number of camels.

عَنْ عُقْبَةَ بْنِ عَامِرٍ، قَالَ خَرَجَ رَسُولُ اللَّهِ صلى الله عليه وسلم وَنَحْنُ فِي الصُّفَّةِ فَقَالَ " أَيُّكُمْ يُحِبُّ أَنْ يَغْدُوَ كُلَّ يَوْمٍ إِلَى بُطْحَانَ أَوْ إِلَى الْعَقِيقِ فَيَأْتِيَ مِنْهُ بِنَاقَتَيْنِ كَوْمَاوَيْنِ فِي غَيْرِ إِثْمٍ وَلاَ قَطْعِ رَحِمٍ " . فَقُلْنَا يَا رَسُولَ اللَّهِ نُحِبُّ ذَلِكَ . قَالَ " أَفَلاَ يَغْدُو أَحَدُكُمْ إِلَى الْمَسْجِدِ فَيَعْلَمَ أَوْ يَقْرَأَ آيَتَيْنِ مِنْ كِتَابِ اللَّهِ عَزَّ وَجَلَّ خَيْرٌ لَهُ مِنْ نَاقَتَيْنِ وَثَلاَثٌ خَيْرٌ لَهُ مِنْ ثَلاَثٍ وَأَرْبَعٌ خَيْرٌ لَهُ مِنْ أَرْبَعٍ وَمِنْ أَعْدَادِهِنَّ مِنَ الإِبِلِ " .

(Saheeh Muslim 803)

8. **A Crown of Honour and Garments of Honour for him; his parents will have beautiful clothes**
9. **Allaah will be Pleased with the person who learns Qur'aan**
10. **Recite and rise in degrees in Jannah**

Abu Hurairah رضي الله عنه said that the Prophet (ﷺ) said:

"The Qur'an shall come on the Day of Judgement and say: 'O Lord! Decorate him." So he is donned with a crown of nobility. Then it says: "O Lord! Give him more!' So he is donned with a suit of nobility. Then it says: "O Lord! Be pleased with him.' So He is pleased with him and says: "Recite and rise up, and be increased in reward with every Ayah.'"

عَنْ أَبِي هُرَيْرَةَ، عَنِ النَّبِيِّ صلى الله عليه وسلم قَالَ " يَجِيءُ الْقُرْآنُ يَوْمَ الْقِيَامَةِ فَيَقُولُ يَا رَبِّ حَلِّهِ فَيُلْبَسُ تَاجَ الْكَرَامَةِ ثُمَّ يَقُولُ يَا رَبِّ زِدْهُ فَيُلْبَسُ حُلَّةَ الْكَرَامَةِ ثُمَّ يَقُولُ يَا رَبِّ ارْضَ عَنْهُ فَيَرْضَى عَنْهُ فَيُقَالُ لَهُ اقْرَأْ وَارْقَ وَتُزَادُ بِكُلِّ آيَةٍ حَسَنَةً " . قَالَ أَبُو عِيسَى هَذَا حَدِيثٌ حَسَنٌ صَحِيحٌ .

(Tirmidhee Hadith 3164)

Abu Hurayrah رضي الله عنه narrated that the Prophet ﷺ said:

"The Qur'aan will come on the Day of Resurrection in the form of a pale man and he will say to (his friend): 'Do you recognize me? I was the one who used to keep you awake at night and made you thirsty at midday. Indeed, every trader will be behind his trade and I am for you today behind every trader.
He will be given the kingdom on his right and eternal life on his left.
A crown of dignity will be placed on his head and his parents will be given two garments to wear worth more than the world and what is in it. They both will say 'O Lord! Where did we get this from?' So it will be said, 'From teaching your child the Qur'aan.'
It will be said to the one who memorized Qur'aan on the Day of Resurrection: Read and ascend in degrees, recite how you used to recite in the World for indeed your place is at the last aayah you have memorized."

يجيء القرآن يوم القيامة كالرجل الشاحب يقول لصاحبه: هل تعرفني؟ أنا الذي كنت أسهر ليلك وأظمئ هواجرك، وإن كل تاجر من وراء تجارته، وأنا لك اليوم من وراء كل تاجر، فيعطى الملك بيمينه والخلد بشماله ويوضع على رأسه تاج الوقار ويكسى

والداه حلتين لا تقوم لهم الدنيا وما فيها، فيقولان: يا رب !أنى لنا هذا؟ فيقال: بتعليم ولدكما القرآن. وإن صاحب القرآن يقال له يوم القيامة: اقرأ وارق في الدرجات ورتل كما كنت ترتل في الدنيا، فإن منزلك عند آخر آية معك. "

(Silsilah Saheehah 2829)

****

Status of the one who has Memorized the Qur'aan:

1. He is from the People of Allaah and His Special Ones

It was narrated that Anas bin Malik رضي الله عنه said:
"The Messenger of Allah صلى الله عليه وسلم said: 'Allah has His own people among mankind.' They said: 'O Messenger of Allah, who are they?' He said: 'The people of the Qur'an, the people of Allah and those who are closest to Him.'"

عَنْ أَنَسِ بْنِ مَالِكٍ، قَالَ قَالَ رَسُولُ اللَّهِ ـ صلى الله عليه وسلم
" إِنَّ لِلَّهِ أَهْلِينَ مِنَ النَّاسِ " . قَالُوا يَا رَسُولَ اللَّهِ مَنْ هُمْ قَالَ " هُمْ أَهْلُ الْقُرْآنِ أَهْلُ اللَّهِ وَخَاصَّتُهُ "

(Ibn Maajah no. 215).

2. He is the Best of People - those who Learn and Teach the Qur'aan

'Uthman رضي الله عنه narrated that the Prophet صلى الله عليه وسلم said,
"The best among you (Muslims) are those who learn the Qur'an and teach it."

عَنْ عُثْمَانَ ـ رضى الله عنه ـ عَنِ النَّبِيِّ صلى الله عليه وسلم قَالَ
"خَيْرُكُمْ مَنْ تَعَلَّمَ الْقُرْآنَ وَعَلَّمَهُ "

(Bukhaaree. no. 5027).

3. He Deserves Honour from the People

Narrated Abu Musa al-Ash'ari رضي الله عنه:

The Prophet (ﷺ) said: Glorifying Allah involves showing honour to a grey-haired Muslim and to one who has memorized the Qur'an, but not to one who acts extravagantly regarding it, or turns away from it, and showing honour to a just ruler.

عَنْ أَبِي مُوسَى الأَشْعَرِيِّ، قَالَ قَالَ رَسُولُ اللَّهِ صلى الله عليه وسلم

" إِنَّ مِنْ إِجْلاَلِ اللَّهِ إِكْرَامَ ذِي الشَّيْبَةِ الْمُسْلِمِ وَحَامِلِ الْقُرْآنِ غَيْرِ الْغَالِي فِيهِ وَالْجَافِي عَنْهُ وَإِكْرَامَ ذِي السُّلْطَانِ الْمُقْسِطِ " .

(Abu Dawood 4843).

4. He has Priority in Leading the Prayer

Abu Mas'ood al-Ansari رضي الله عنه reported Allah's Messenger (ﷺ) as saying:

The one who is most versed in Allah's Book should act as Imam for the people, but If they are equally versed in reciting it, then the one who has most knowledge regarding Sunnah if they are equal regarding the Sunnah, then the earliest one to emigrate; it they emigrated at the same time, then the earliest one to embrace Islam. No man must lead another in prayer where (the latter) has authority, or sit in his place of honour in his house, without his permission. Ashajj in his narration used the word," age" in place of" Islam".

عَنْ أَبِي مَسْعُودٍ الأَنْصَارِيِّ، قَالَ قَالَ رَسُولُ اللَّهِ صلى الله عليه وسلم

"يَؤُمُّ الْقَوْمَ أَقْرَؤُهُمْ لِكِتَابِ اللَّهِ فَإِنْ كَانُوا فِي الْقِرَاءَةِ سَوَاءً فَأَعْلَمُهُمْ بِالسُّنَّةِ فَإِنْ كَانُوا فِي السُّنَّةِ سَوَاءً فَأَقْدَمُهُمْ هِجْرَةً فَإِنْ كَانُوا فِي الْهِجْرَةِ سَوَاءً فَأَقْدَمُهُمْ سِلْمًا وَلاَ يَؤُمَّنَّ الرَّجُلُ الرَّجُلَ فِي سُلْطَانِهِ وَلاَ يَقْعُدْ فِي بَيْتِهِ عَلَى تَكْرِمَتِهِ إِلاَّ بِإِذْنِهِ " .

قَالَ الأَشَجُّ فِي رِوَايَتِهِ مَكَانَ سِلْمًا سِنًّا .

(Saheeh Muslim 673)

5. **He is given precedence to be appointed Leadership Roles due to his knowledge of the Qur'aan**

'Aamir bin Waathila reported that Naafi' bin 'Abd al-Haarith met 'Umar at 'Usfaan and 'Umar had employed him as a collector in Makkah. He ('Umar) said to him (Naafi'): Who have you appointed as collector over the people of the valley? He said: Ibn Abza. He said: Who is Ibn Abza? He said: He is one of our freed slaves. He ('Umar) said: So you have appointed a freed slave over them. He said: He is well versed In the Book of Allah, the Exalted and Great, and he is well versed in the commandments and injunctions (of the Shari'ah). 'Umar said: So the Prophet (ﷺ) said: By this Book, Allah would exalt some peoples and degrade others.

عَنْ عَامِرِ بْنِ وَاثِلَةَ، أَنَّ نَافِعَ بْنَ عَبْدِ الْحَارِثِ، لَقِيَ عُمَرَ بِعُسْفَانَ وَكَانَ عُمَرُ
يَسْتَعْمِلُهُ عَلَى مَكَّةَ فَقَالَ مَنِ اسْتَعْمَلْتَ عَلَى أَهْلِ الْوَادِي فَقَالَ ابْنَ أَبْزَى .
قَالَ وَمَنِ ابْنُ أَبْزَى قَالَ مَوْلًى مِنْ مَوَالِينَا . قَالَ فَاسْتَخْلَفْتَ عَلَيْهِمْ مَوْلًى
قَالَ إِنَّهُ قَارِئٌ لِكِتَابِ اللَّهِ عَزَّ وَجَلَّ وَإِنَّهُ عَالِمٌ بِالْفَرَائِضِ .
قَالَ عُمَرُ أَمَا إِنَّ نَبِيَّكُمْ صلى الله عليه وسلم قَدْ قَالَ
" إِنَّ اللَّهَ يَرْفَعُ بِهَذَا الْكِتَابِ أَقْوَامًا وَيَضَعُ بِهِ آخَرِينَ " .

(Saheeh Muslim 817a)

6. **He is placed first into the grave if there is more than one person to a grave**

Narrated Jabir bin `Abdullah رضي الله عنه:

The Prophet (ﷺ) collected every two martyrs of Uhud in one piece of cloth, then he would ask, "Which of them knew more of the Qur'an?" When one of them was pointed out for him, he would put that one first in the grave and say, "I will be a witness on these on the Day of Resurrection."

عَنْ جَابِرِ بْنِ عَبْدِ اللَّهِ ـ رضى الله عنهما ـ قَالَ كَانَ النَّبِيُّ صلى الله عليه
وسلم يَجْمَعُ بَيْنَ الرَّجُلَيْنِ مِنْ قَتْلَى أُحُدٍ فِي ثَوْبٍ وَاحِدٍ ثُمَّ يَقُولُ
" أَيُّهُمْ أَكْثَرُ أَخْذًا لِلْقُرْآنِ ". فَإِذَا أُشِيرَ لَهُ إِلَى أَحَدِهِمَا قَدَّمَهُ فِي اللَّحْدِ
وَقَالَ " أَنَا شَهِيدٌ عَلَى هَؤُلاَءِ يَوْمَ الْقِيَامَةِ

(Saheeh al-Bukhaaree 1343)

7. He is carrying the Flag of Islaam

"The one who has memorized the Qur'aan is carrying the flag of Islaam. It is not befitting for him to engage in useless pastimes with those who engage in useless pastimes, nor to be negligent with those who are negligent, nor to engage in useless talk with those who engage in useless talk. This comes out of respecting and exalting the rights of the Qur'aan."
Saying by Fudayl ibn Iyaad. 'At Tibyaan fee Aadaab Hamalatil Qur'aan.' P44.

General Reminders about the Qur'aan

1.

وَلَقَدْ يَسَّرْنَا الْقُرْآنَ لِلذِّكْرِ فَهَلْ مِن مُّدَّكِرٍ

And We have indeed made the Qur'ân easy to understand and remember; then is there anyone who will remember (or receive admonition)?

al Qamr [54:17]

2.

{قُلْ بِفَضْلِ اللَّهِ وَبِرَحْمَتِهِ فَبِذَٰلِكَ فَلْيَفْرَحُوا هُوَ خَيْرٌ مِّمَّا يَجْمَعُونَ}

Say: "In the Bounty of Allah, and in His Mercy (i.e. Islam and the Qur'an); -therein let them rejoice." That is better than (the wealth) they amass.

[Yoonus :58]

3. Imaam Nawawee رحمه الله said,
"The Salaf would not teach someone hadeeth nor fiqh until they had memorized the Qur'aan." (Majmoo' 1/69).

4. Al Khateeb al Baghdaadee رحمه الله said,
"A student should start by memorizing Allaah's Book as it is the most honourable of sciences and the foremost to prioritise."
(al Jaami' li Akhlaaq ar Raawee wa Adaab as Saamee 1/106).

5. Musa bin 'Uqba رضي الله عنه said,
" When one who had committed the Qur'an to memory (or who is familiar with it) gets up (for night prayer) and recites it night and day, it remains fresh in his mind, but if he does not get up (for prayer and thus does not recite it) he forgets it."

حَدِيثِ مُوسَى بْنِ عُقْبَةَ " وَإِذَا قَامَ صَاحِبُ الْقُرْآنِ فَقَرَأَهُ بِاللَّيْلِ وَالنَّهَارِ ذَكَرَهُ وَإِذَا لَمْ يَقُمْ بِهِ نَسِيَهُ "

(Saheeh Muslim 789 b)

6. Narrated Abu Huraira:

Allah's Messenger (ﷺ) said, "There is no envy except in two circumstances: A man whom Allah has taught the Qur'an and he recites it during the hours of the night and during the hours of the day, and his neighbour listens to him and says, 'I wish I had been given what has been given to so-and-so, so that I might do what he does; and a man whom Allah has given wealth and he spends it on what is just and right, whereupon another man may say, 'I wish I had been given what so-and-so has been given, for then I would do what he does."

عَنْ أَبِي هُرَيْرَةَ، أَنَّ رَسُولَ اللَّهِ صلى الله عليه وسلم قَالَ " لاَ حَسَدَ إِلاَّ فِي اثْنَتَيْنِ رَجُلٌ عَلَّمَهُ اللَّهُ الْقُرْآنَ فَهُوَ يَتْلُوهُ آنَاءَ اللَّيْلِ وَآنَاءَ النَّهَارِ فَسَمِعَهُ جَارٌ لَهُ فَقَالَ لَيْتَنِي أُوتِيتُ مِثْلَ مَا أُوتِيَ فُلاَنٌ فَعَمِلْتُ مِثْلَ مَا يَعْمَلُ، وَرَجُلٌ آتَاهُ اللَّهُ مَالاً فَهْوَ يُهْلِكُهُ فِي الْحَقِّ فَقَالَ رَجُلٌ لَيْتَنِي أُوتِيتُ مِثْلَ مَا أُوتِيَ فُلاَنٌ فَعَمِلْتُ مِثْلَ مَا يَعْمَلُ ".

Saheeh al-Bukhaaree 5026

7. It has been narrated on the authority of Sulaiman bin Yasar who said:
I heard the Messenger of Allah (ﷺ) say: The first of men (whose case) will be decided on the Day of Judgment will be a man who died as a martyr. ....Then will be brought forward a man who acquired knowledge and imparted it (to others) and recited the Qur'an. He will be brought and Allah will make him recount His blessings and he will recount them (and admit having enjoyed them in his lifetime). Then will Allah ask: What did you do (to requite these blessings)? He will say: I acquired knowledge and disseminated it and recited the Qur'an seeking Your pleasure. Allah will say: You have told a lie. You acquired knowledge so that you might be called" a scholar," and you recited the Qur'an so that it might be said:" He is a Qaari" and such has been said. Then orders will be passed against him and he shall be dragged with his face downward and cast into the Fire. Then will be brought a man whom Allah had made abundantly rich and had granted every kind of wealth..........

عَنْ سُلَيْمَانَ بْنِ يَسَارٍ سَمِعْتُ رَسُولَ اللَّهِ صلى الله عليه وسلم يَقُولُ " إِنَّ أَوَّلَ النَّاسِ يُقْضَى يَوْمَ الْقِيَامَةِ عَلَيْهِ رَجُلٌ اسْتُشْهِدَ .... وَرَجُلٌ تَعَلَّمَ الْعِلْمَ وَعَلَّمَهُ وَقَرَأَ الْقُرْآنَ فَأُتِيَ بِهِ فَعَرَّفَهُ نِعَمَهُ فَعَرَفَهَا قَالَ فَمَا عَمِلْتَ فِيهَا قَالَ تَعَلَّمْتُ الْعِلْمَ وَعَلَّمْتُهُ وَقَرَأْتُ فِيكَ الْقُرْآنَ . قَالَ كَذَبْتَ وَلَكِنَّكَ تَعَلَّمْتَ الْعِلْمَ لِيُقَالَ عَالِمٌ . وَقَرَأْتَ الْقُرْآنَ لِيُقَالَ هُوَ قَارِئٌ . فَقَدْ قِيلَ ثُمَّ أُمِرَ بِهِ فَسُحِبَ عَلَى وَجْهِهِ حَتَّى أُلْقِيَ فِي النَّارِ . وَرَجُلٌ وَسَّعَ اللَّهُ عَلَيْهِ وَأَعْطَاهُ مِنْ أَصْنَافِ الْمَالِ كُلِّهِ ...." .

(Saheeh Muslim 1905 a)

Summary

Rewards for the one who has Memorized the Qur'aan

1. A person who recites the Qur'aan and learns it by heart will be with the angels
2. The memorizer of the Qur'aan will be saved from the fire.
3. The Qur'aan will intercede on the Day of Resurrection
4. Sooratul Baqarah and Aali 'Imraan will come as two clouds, flocks of birds or two shades.
5. He will receive good deeds for each letter he reads of the Qur'aan.
6. He will receive the same reward as those he has taught Qur'aan
7. Each aayaah learned is better than getting a big humped she-camel.
8. A crown of honour (Taaj al Waqaar/Taaj al Karaamah) and garments of honour for him; his parents will have beautiful clothes
9. Allaah will be pleased with the person who learns Qur'aan
10. He will recite and rise in degrees in Jannah

Status of the one who has Memorized the Qur'aan:

1. He is from the People of Allaah and His special ones
2. He is the Best of people - those who learn and teach the Qur'aan.
3. He deserves honour from the people.
4. He has priority in leading the prayer.
5. He is given precedence to be appointed leadership roles due to his knowledge of the Qur'aan.
6. He is placed first into the grave closer to the qiblah if there is more than one person to a grave.
7. He is carrying the flag of Islaam.

Rewards for Parents

Reward for the Memorizer	Reward for his/her Parents
	“O Lord where did we get this from?” “For teaching your child the Qur’aan”
Crown of dignity and honour تاج الوَقار	
Clothes of nobility and honour حُلة الكرامة	The most beautiful clothes حُلتين لا تقوم لهم الدنيا وما فيها

NB. There is a weak hadeeth that mentions the parents of the memorizer having a crown.

Mu'adh al-Juhani reported the Messenger of Allah (ﷺ) as saying:
If anyone recites the Qur'an and acts according to its content, on the Day of Judgement his parents will be given to wear a crown whose light is better than the light of the sun in the dwellings of this world if it were among you. So what do you think of him who acts according to this?

حَدَّثَنَا أَحْمَدُ بْنُ عَمْرِو بْنِ السَّرْحِ، أَخْبَرَنَا ابْنُ وَهْبٍ، أَخْبَرَنِي يَحْيَى بْنُ أَيُّوبَ، عَنْ زَبَّانَ بْنِ فَائِدٍ، عَنْ سَهْلِ بْنِ مُعَاذٍ الْجُهَنِيِّ، عَنْ أَبِيهِ، أَنَّ رَسُولَ اللَّهِ صلى الله عليه وسلم قَالَ " مَنْ قَرَأَ الْقُرْآنَ وَعَمِلَ بِمَا فِيهِ أُلْبِسَ وَالِدَاهُ تَاجًا يَوْمَ الْقِيَامَةِ ضَوْؤُهُ أَحْسَنُ مِنْ ضَوْءِ الشَّمْسِ فِي بُيُوتِ الدُّنْيَا لَوْ كَانَتْ فِيكُمْ فَمَا ظَنُّكُمْ بِالَّذِي عَمِلَ بِهَذَا " .

Sunan Abi Dawud 1453 Graded as a weak Hadeeth - Da'eef by Shaykh Al-Albanee.

Sources:

The Noble Qur’aan
Ad Daleel ila ta’leem Kitaab Allaahi al Jaleel (A guide to Teaching Allaah’s Magnificent Book) by Shaykh Al-Albaani’s daughters Hassaanah and Sukaynah.
Ahaadeeth from www.sunnah.com and www.hadithportal.com

Expressions of Congratulations and Encouragement for Memorizing the Noble Qur'aan[1]

by Shaykh 'AbdurRazzaaq 'Abdul Muhsin al-Badr

كملت الحفظ ما شاء الله

Have you completed your memorization?

Alhamdulillaahالحمد لله

Allaah accept it, congratulations (blessings)الله يتقبل مبارك

How old are you? I'm 18 years old١٨ كم عمرك؟ أنا

What's your good name?اسم الكريم؟ محمد ناصر الخاجة

يلى بسم الله ما شاء الله قبل شهر كملت حفظ القرآن؟ إي الحمد لله البركة

OK, bismillaah. Maa shaa Allaah a month ago you completed your hifdth of the Qur'aan? Yes alhamdulillaah blessings.

البركة جعله الله حجة لك ونفعك بالقرآن ورفعك ما شاء الله

أنت قدوة للشباب إن شاء الله يستفيدون من همتك ونشاطك

Allaah make it (the Qur'aan) a proof for you, may you benefit from it and raise in degrees.

An example for the youth to benefit from your motivation and hard work.

OK beginفضل

What shall I read?أقرأ أي شيء أنا؟

Shall I specify something or do you want to read?أحدد لك أنا ولا أنت بتقرأ؟

I don't knowما أعرف

Shall I specify or do you want to choose something?أحدد لك ولا أنت بتختار إلي تبي؟

I'll chooseأنا بأختار

تختار؟ خلاص مرة أنت تختار ومرة أنا أختار. ابدأ بما أنت تختار الآن

You will choose? Ok you choose once and I'll choose. Start with what you choose now

Inshaa Allaahإن شاء الله

وَسِيقَ الَّذِينَ كَفَرُوا إِلَىٰ جَهَنَّمَ زُمَرًا ۖ حَتَّىٰ إِذَا جَاءُوهَا فُتِحَتْ أَبْوَابُهَا وَقَالَ لَهُمْ
خَزَنَتُهَا أَلَمْ يَأْتِكُمْ رُسُلٌ مِّنكُمْ يَتْلُونَ عَلَيْكُمْ آيَاتِ رَبِّكُمْ وَيُنذِرُونَكُمْ لِقَاءَ يَوْمِكُمْ هَٰذَا ۚ
قَالُوا بَلَىٰ وَلَٰكِنْ حَقَّتْ كَلِمَةُ الْعَذَابِ عَلَى الْكَافِرِينَ (71) قِيلَ ادْخُلُوا أَبْوَابَ جَهَنَّمَ
خَالِدِينَ فِيهَا ۖ فَبِئْسَ مَثْوَى الْمُتَكَبِّرِينَ (72) وَسِيقَ الَّذِينَ اتَّقَوْا رَبَّهُمْ إِلَى الْجَنَّةِ

---

[1] Transcribed and translated by Umm 'AbdirRahmaan

زُمَرًا ۖ حَتَّىٰ إِذَا جَاءُوهَا وَفُتِحَتْ أَبْوَابُهَا وَقَالَ لَهُمْ خَزَنَتُهَا سَلَامٌ عَلَيْكُمْ طِبْتُمْ
فَادْخُلُوهَا خَالِدِينَ (73) وَقَالُوا الْحَمْدُ لِلَّهِ الَّذِي صَدَقَنَا وَعْدَهُ وَأَوْرَثَنَا الْأَرْضَ
نَتَبَوَّأُ مِنَ الْجَنَّةِ حَيْثُ نَشَاءُ ۖ فَنِعْمَ أَجْرُ الْعَامِلِينَ (74) وَتَرَى الْمَلَائِكَةَ حَافِّينَ مِنْ
حَوْلِ الْعَرْشِ يُسَبِّحُونَ بِحَمْدِ رَبِّهِمْ ۖ وَقُضِيَ بَيْنَهُم بِالْحَقِّ وَقِيلَ الْحَمْدُ لِلَّهِ رَبِّ
الْعَالَمِينَ

71. And those who disbelieved will be driven to Hell in groups, till, when they reach it, the gates thereof will be opened (suddenly like a prison at the arrival of the prisoners). And its keepers will say, "Did not the Messengers come to you from yourselves, reciting to you the Verses of your Lord, and warning you of the Meeting of this Day of yours?" They will say: "Yes, but the Word of torment has been justified against the disbelievers!"

72. It will be said (to them): "Enter you the gates of Hell, to abide therein. And (indeed) what an evil abode of the arrogant!"

73. And those who kept their duty to their Lord will be led to Paradise in groups, till, when they reach it, and its gates will be opened (before their arrival for their reception) and its keepers will say: *Salamun 'Alaikum* (peace be upon you)! You have done well, so enter here to abide therein."

74. And they will say: "All the praises and thanks be to Allah Who has fulfilled His Promise to us and has made us inherit (this) land. We can dwell in Paradise where we will; how excellent a reward for the (pious good) workers!"

75. And you will see the angels surrounding the Throne (of Allah) from all round, glorifying the praises of their Lord (Allah). And they (all the creatures) will be judged with truth, and it will be said. All the praises and thanks be to Allah, the Lord of the *'Alamin* (mankind, jinns and all that exists)."

[Zumar 39:71-75]

******

ما شاء الله ما شاء الله ما شاء الله الله يزيدك. اقرأ من قوله تعالى:

إِنَّ هَٰذَا الْقُرْآنَ يَهْدِي لِلَّتِي هِيَ أَقْوَمُ وَيُبَشِّرُ الْمُؤْمِنِينَ الَّذِينَ يَعْمَلُونَ الصَّالِحَاتِ أَنَّ
لَهُمْ أَجْرًا كَبِيرًا (9) وَأَنَّ الَّذِينَ لَا يُؤْمِنُونَ بِالْآخِرَةِ أَعْتَدْنَا لَهُمْ عَذَابًا أَلِيمًا (10)

وَيَدْعُ الْإِنسَانُ بِالشَّرِّ دُعَاءَهُ بِالْخَيْرِ ۖ وَكَانَ الْإِنسَانُ عَجُولًا (11) وَجَعَلْنَا اللَّيْلَ
وَالنَّهَارَ آيَتَيْنِ ۖ فَمَحَوْنَا آيَةَ اللَّيْلِ وَجَعَلْنَا آيَةَ النَّهَارِ مُبْصِرَةً لِّتَبْتَغُوا فَضْلًا مِّن رَّبِّكُمْ
وَلِتَعْلَمُوا عَدَدَ السِّنِينَ وَالْحِسَابَ ۚ وَكُلَّ شَيْءٍ فَصَّلْنَاهُ تَفْصِيلًا (12) وَكُلَّ إِنسَانٍ
أَلْزَمْنَاهُ طَائِرَهُ فِي عُنُقِهِ ۖ وَنُخْرِجُ لَهُ يَوْمَ الْقِيَامَةِ كِتَابًا يَلْقَاهُ مَنشُورًا (13) اقْرَأْ
كِتَابَكَ كَفَىٰ بِنَفْسِكَ الْيَوْمَ عَلَيْكَ حَسِيبًا (14) مَّنِ اهْتَدَىٰ فَإِنَّمَا يَهْتَدِي لِنَفْسِهِ ۖ وَمَن
ضَلَّ فَإِنَّمَا يَضِلُّ عَلَيْهَا ۚ وَلَا تَزِرُ وَازِرَةٌ وِزْرَ أُخْرَىٰ ۗ وَمَا كُنَّا مُعَذِّبِينَ حَتَّىٰ نَبْعَثَ
رَسُولًا

9. Verily, this Qur'an guides to that which is most just and right and gives glad tidings to the believers (in the Oneness of Allah and His Messenger, Muhammad , etc.). who work deeds of righteousness, that they shall have a great reward (Paradise).
10. And that those who believe not in the Hereafter (i.e. they disbelieve that they will be recompensed for what they did in this world, good or bad, etc.), for them We have prepared a painful torment (Hell).
11. And man invokes (Allah) for evil as he invokes (Allah) for good and man is ever hasty [i.e., if he is angry with somebody, he invokes (saying): "O Allah! Curse him, etc." and that one should not do, but one should be patient].
12. And We have appointed the night and the day as two *Ayat* (signs etc.). Then, We have made dark the sign of the night while We have made the sign of day illuminating, that you may seek bounty from your Lord, and that you may know the number of the years and the reckoning. And We have explained everything (in detail) with full explanation.
13. And We have fastened every man's deeds to his neck, and on the Day of Resurrection, We shall bring out for him a book which he will find wide open.
14. (It will be said to him): "Read your book. You yourself are sufficient as a reckoner against you this Day."
15. Whoever goes right, then he goes right only for the benefit of his own self. And whoever goes astray, then he goes astray to his own loss. No one laden with burdens can bear another's burden. And We never punish until We have sent a Messenger (to give warning).
[Israa 17:9-15]

****

وَسَارِعُوا إِلَىٰ مَغْفِرَةٍ مِّن رَّبِّكُمْ وَجَنَّةٍ عَرْضُهَا السَّمَاوَاتُ وَالْأَرْضُ
أُعِدَّتْ لِلْمُتَّقِينَ (133) الَّذِينَ يُنفِقُونَ فِي السَّرَّاءِ وَالضَّرَّاءِ وَالْكَاظِمِينَ
الْغَيْظَ وَالْعَافِينَ عَنِ النَّاسِ ۗ وَاللَّهُ يُحِبُّ الْمُحْسِنِينَ) 134 (وَالَّذِينَ إِذَا
فَعَلُوا فَاحِشَةً أَوْ ظَلَمُوا أَنفُسَهُمْ ذَكَرُوا اللَّهَ فَاسْتَغْفَرُوا لِذُنُوبِهِمْ وَمَن يَغْفِرُ
الذُّنُوبَ إِلَّا اللَّهُ وَلَمْ يُصِرُّوا عَلَىٰ مَا فَعَلُوا وَهُمْ يَعْلَمُونَ) 135 (أُولَٰئِكَ
جَزَاؤُهُم مَّغْفِرَةٌ مِّن رَّبِّهِمْ وَجَنَّاتٌ تَجْرِي مِن تَحْتِهَا الْأَنْهَارُ خَالِدِينَ
فِيهَا ۚ وَنِعْمَ أَجْرُ الْعَامِلِينَ

133. And march forth in the way (which leads to) forgiveness from your Lord, and for Paradise as wide as are the heavens and the earth, prepared for *Al-Muttaqun* (the pious - see V.2:2).
134. Those who spend [in Allah's Cause - deeds of charity, alms, etc.] in prosperity and in adversity, who repress anger, and who pardon men; verily, Allah loves *Al-Muhsinun* (the good-doers).
135. And those who, when they have committed *Fahishah* (illegal sexual intercourse etc.) or wronged themselves with evil, remember Allah and ask forgiveness for their sins; - and none can forgive sins but Allah - And do not persist in what (wrong) they have done, while they know.
136. For such, the reward is Forgiveness from their Lord, and Gardens with rivers flowing underneath (Paradise), wherein they shall abide forever. How excellent is this reward for the doers (who do righteous deeds according to Allah's Orders). [Aali ‘Imraan 3:133-136]

ما شاء الله ما شاء الله بارك الله فيك

Maa shaa Allaah BaarakAllaahu feek
(Shaykh kisses the boy)

الله يزيدك ويثبتك ويحفظك إن شاء الله قدوة للشباب للخير وبركة

Allaah increase you and make you firm. Allaah preserve you. Inshaa Allaah you will be a role model for the youth for good and blessings.

سرنا والله العلم الغانم والاتقان بالحفظ

Your knowledge that you have gained and your precision in memorizing has pleased us.

زادك الله فضلا وتوفيقا وبركة بارك الله فيك

Allaah increase you in grace, success and blessings. BaarakAllaah feek.

Common Arab Expressions of Congratulations

Here are a few common expressions the Arabs use when someone has been blessed to complete the whole Qur'aan off by heart. They are not from the sunnah, just everyday expressions of happiness.

1.

ألف مبروك حفظ القران الكريم
أسأل الله العلي القدير أن يثبته في صدرك وأن يكون حجة لك لا عليك. وأن يرفعك به الدرجات في الجنان ووالديك

Congratulations upon memorizing the Noble Qur'aan!
I ask Allaah The High, The All-Able to make it firm in your heart and that it be a proof for you and not against you.
I ask that Allaah raises you and your parents in rank by it in Jannah.
Aameen!

****

2.

هنئيا لك فقد خصك الرحمن بحفظ كتابه

Congratulations! The Most Merciful has chosen you to memorize His Book

****

3.

جعله الله حجة لك ونفعك بالقرآن ورفعك ما شاء الله

Allaah make it (the Qur'aan) a proof for you, may you benefit from it and raise in degrees.

4.

الله يزيدك ويثبتك ويحفظك

Allaah increase you and make you firm. Allaah preserve you.

5.

زادك الله فضلا وتوفيقا وبركة بارك الله فيك

Allaah increase you in grace, success and blessings. BaarakAllaah feek.

6.

To my precious pearl, my little one, ________________

How can we start to congratulate you when the words are flying out of happiness to give you glad tidings for Allaah's Grace upon you?

How can we express our feelings to ask for Allaah to bless your perseverance and enormous efforts?

Well done for this honour of memorizing the whole Qur'aan off by heart.

Allaah, al Mawlaa the Supporter, bless your efforts and fulfil your wishes.

Allaah grant you a crown of honour on the Day of Resurrection.

All praises are for Allaah by whose blessings good deeds are accomplished.

I wish you more success and progress in this Life and the Next.

We are proud of you my precious one!

أيتها اللؤلؤة الثمينة

بنيتي

من أين نبدأ والحروف تتطاير فرحا لتهنئتك

لتزف لك تباشير السعادة والفضل الإلهي

أم كيف نصوغ مشاعرنا لنبارك مثابرتك واجتهادك

فهنيئا لك هذا الشرف و وسام حفظ القرآن كاملا

فليبارك المولى مساعيك ويحققك كل أمانيك وتلبسين تاج الوقار يوم القيامة

الحمدلله الذي بنعمته تتم الصالحات

وأتمنى لك مزيدا من التقدم و التفوق في الدنيا والآخرة

نحن فخورون بك يا غاليتي!

****

Ruling on holding a celebration for someone who has memorized the Qur'aan

Question: Is it permissible to hold a celebration for the one who has completed the memorization of the Qur'aan by bringing food and the like?

Answer by Shaykh Saalih Fawzaan حفظه الله:

There is no problem with this. This is from encouraging the good. 'Umar, I think, when he memorized Sooratul Baqarah, he held a 'waleemah' gathering with food. There is no problem in this, encouraging good from happiness and delight at something good.

Source in Arabic: https://youtu.be/VNOhEJZzF7M

Shaykh Al-Albaani رحمه الله mentioned that there is nothing specific from the sunnah to celebrate after memorizing the Qur'aan. (Not like marriage or newborn where there is evidence to celebrate from the sunnah). The narration about 'Umar رضي الله عنه holding a waleemah after memorizing may not be authentic.

Shaykh 'Ubayd al Jaabiri حفظه الله said that if it is not extravagant and it is just a small party for family and a few friends to show their gratitude and to make du'aa for the one who has memorized Qur'aan that he acts upon it and benefits from it so that he becomes from Allaah's people then it is allowed. (It should not be extravagant and like a wedding party).

See full answer in Arabic - https://youtu.be/cYIfprUArWk

A Few of my Teaching Resources:

1. Qur'aan Teacher Resources www.quraanteacherresources.blogspot.com
2. Learn the Vocabulary of the Qur'aan www.learn-quran-vocab.blogspot.com
3. Daily Qur'aan Reading Schedule www.dailyquraanreading.blogspot.com
4. Study Juz Amma www.studyjuzamma.blogspot.com
5. Learn Suratul Baqarah www.suratulbaqarah.blogspot.com

Telegram Channels: Https//t.me/dailyQuraanreading

Scan the QR code for the books on Amazon or search 'Tara Hashim'

	Book Titles	Author/level/version
1	An Explanation of the Creed of Muhammad Ibn 'Abdil Wahhaab	By Shaykh Saalih Al-Fawzaan
2	Workbook to go with No. 1 above.	
3	Learn the Beautiful Names of Allaah	Explanation Sh. AbdurRazzaaq
4	Learn the Beautiful Names of Allaah	Coursebook
5	Learn the Beautiful Names of Allaah	Workbook
6	Learn the Beautiful Names of Allaah	Research book
7	Learn the Words of the Qur'aan	level 1
8	Learn the Words of the Qur'aan	level 2
9	Strategic Tips for Qur'aan Memorization	
10	Let's Learn About Arabic Calligraphy	
11	Saudi Souvenirs Colouring Book	
12	Mistakes Record Notebook for Memorization or Recitation	Version A labelled Surah names
13	Mistakes Record Notebook for Memorization or Recitation	Version B blank names
14	Hajj Activity Pack	
15	Quranic Vocabulary Notebook	
16	The Mothers of the Believers – The Prophet's ﷺWives رضي الله عنهن	
17	Rewards and Status for Memorizing the Qur'aan	

Made in the USA
Middletown, DE
20 October 2022

13179875R00017